# Chicken

## Everyday recipes to enjoy

# chicken-noodle soup

## ingredients

**SERVES 4–6**

2 skinless chicken breasts

2 litres/3$^1$/$_2$ pints water

1 onion, with skin left on,
    cut in half

1 large garlic clove, cut in half

1-cm/$^1$/$_2$-inch piece fresh
    ginger, peeled and sliced

4 black peppercorns, lightly
    crushed

4 cloves

2 star anise

salt and pepper

1 carrot, peeled

1 celery stalk, chopped

100 g/3$^1$/$_2$ oz baby corn,
    cut in half lengthways
    and chopped

2 spring onions, finely
    shredded

115 g/4 oz dried rice
    vermicelli noodles

## method

**1** Put the chicken breasts and water in a saucepan over high heat and bring to the boil. Lower the heat to its lowest setting and simmer, skimming the surface until no more foam rises. Add the onion, garlic, ginger, peppercorns, cloves, star anise and a pinch of salt and continue to simmer for 20 minutes, or until the chicken is tender and cooked through. Meanwhile, grate the carrot along its length on the coarse side of a grater so you get long, thin strips.

**2** Strain the chicken, reserving about 1.2 litres/2 pints stock, but discarding any flavouring ingredients. (At this point you can let the stock cool and refrigerate overnight, so any fat solidifies and can be lifted off and discarded.) Return the stock to the rinsed-out pan with the carrot, celery, baby corn and spring onions and bring to the boil. Boil until the baby corn are almost tender, then add the noodles and continue boiling for 2 minutes.

**3** Meanwhile, chop the chicken, add it to the pan and continue cooking for about 1 minute until the chicken is reheated and the noodles are soft. Add seasoning.

# chicken liver pâté

## ingredients

**MAKES 8–10 SLICES**

175 g/6 oz unsalted butter

500 g/1 lb 2 oz chicken livers,
   thawed if frozen,
   and trimmed

1/2 tbsp sunflower oil

2 shallots, finely chopped

2 large garlic cloves, finely
   chopped

2 1/2 tbsp Madeira or brandy

2 tbsp double cream

1 tsp dried thyme

1/4 tsp ground allspice

salt and pepper

toasted brioche slices and
   mixed salad leaves,
   to serve

## method

**1** Melt 25 g/1 oz of the butter in a large frying pan over medium–high heat. Add the chicken livers and stir for 5 minutes, or until they are brown on the outside, but still slightly pink in the centres. Work in batches, if necessary, to avoid overcrowding the pan.

**2** Transfer the livers and their cooking juices to a food processor. Melt another 25 g/1 oz of the butter with the oil in the pan. Add the shallots and garlic and sauté, stirring frequently, for 2–3 minutes, until the shallots are soft, but not brown.

**3** Add the Madeira to the pan and scrape up any cooking juices from the base. Stir in the cream, then the thyme, allspice, salt and pepper. Pour this mixture, with the cooking juices, into the food processor with the livers. Add the remaining butter, cut into small pieces.

**4** Whiz the mixture in the food processor until smooth. Taste, and adjust the seasoning if necessary. Let the mixture cool slightly, then scrape into a serving bowl and set aside to allow the pâté to cool completely.

**5** Serve immediately, or cover and store in the refrigerator for up to 3 days and let stand at room temperature for 30 minutes before serving. Serve with hot toasted brioche and mixed salad leaves.

# soy chicken wings

## ingredients

**SERVES 3–4**

250 g/9 oz chicken wings,
   defrosted if frozen

250 ml/8 fl oz water

1 tbsp sliced spring onion

2.5-cm/1-inch piece of fresh
   ginger, cut into 4 slices

2 tbsp light soy sauce

$^1/_2$ tsp dark soy sauce

1 star anise

1 tsp sugar

## method

**1** Wash and dry the chicken wings. In a small saucepan, bring the water to the boil, then add the chicken, spring onion and ginger and bring back to the boil.

**2** Add the remaining ingredients, then cover and simmer for 30 minutes.

**3** Using a slotted spoon, remove the chicken wings from any remaining liquid and serve hot.

# chicken, cheese & rocket salad

## ingredients

**SERVES 4**

150 g/5½ oz rocket leaves

2 celery stalks, trimmed
and sliced

½ cucumber, sliced

2 spring onions, trimmed
and sliced

2 tbsp chopped
fresh parsley

25 g/1 oz walnut pieces

350 g/12 oz boneless roast
chicken, sliced

125 g/4½ oz Stilton cheese,
cubed

handful of seedless red
grapes, cut in
half (optional)

salt and pepper

### dressing

2 tbsp olive oil

1 tbsp sherry vinegar

1 tsp Dijon mustard

1 tbsp chopped
mixed herbs

## method

**1** Wash the rocket leaves, pat dry with kitchen paper and put them into a large salad bowl. Add the celery, cucumber, spring onions, parsley and walnuts and mix together well. Transfer onto a large serving platter. Arrange the chicken slices over the salad, then scatter over the cheese. Add the red grapes, if using. Season well with salt and pepper.

**2** To make the dressing, put all the ingredients into a screw-top jar and shake well. Alternatively, put them into a bowl and mix together well. Drizzle the dressing over the salad and serve.

# cajun chicken salad

## ingredients

**SERVES 4**

4 skinless, boneless chicken
   breasts, about 140 g/
   5 oz each

4 tsp Cajun seasoning

2 tsp corn oil (optional)

1 ripe mango, peeled, stoned
   and cut into thick slices

200 g/7 oz mixed salad leaves

1 red onion, thinly sliced and
   cut in half

175 g/6 oz cooked beetroot,
   diced

85 g/3 oz radishes, sliced

55 g/2 oz walnut halves

4 tbsp walnut oil

1–2 tsp Dijon mustard

1 tbsp lemon juice

salt and pepper

2 tbsp sesame seeds

## method

**1** Make 3 diagonal slashes across each chicken breast. Put the chicken into a shallow dish and sprinkle all over with the Cajun seasoning. Cover and chill for at least 30 minutes.

**2** When ready to cook, brush a griddle pan with the corn oil, if using. Heat over high heat until very hot and a few drops of water sprinkled into the pan sizzle immediately. Add the chicken and cook for 7–8 minutes on each side, or until thoroughly cooked. If still slightly pink in the centre, cook a little longer. Remove the chicken and set aside.

**3** Add the mango slices to the pan and cook for 2 minutes on each side. Remove from the pan and set aside.

**4** Meanwhile, arrange the salad leaves in a salad bowl, reserving a few for a garnish, and sprinkle over the onion, beetroot, radishes and walnut halves.

**5** Put the walnut oil, mustard, lemon juice, salt and pepper in a screw-top jar and shake until well blended. Pour over the salad and sprinkle with the sesame seeds.

**6** Arrange the mango and the salad on a serving plate, top with the chicken and garnish with the reserved salad leaves.

# chicken wraps

## ingredients

**SERVES 4**

150 ml/5 fl oz low-fat plain
  yogurt

1 tbsp wholegrain mustard

pepper

280 g/10 oz cooked skinless,
  boneless chicken
  breast, diced

140 g/5 oz iceberg lettuce,
  finely shredded

85 g/3 oz cucumber,
  thinly sliced

2 celery stalks, sliced

85 g/3 oz black seedless
  grapes, halved

8 x 20-cm/8-inch soft flour
  tortillas or 4 x 25-cm/
  10-inch soft flour tortillas

## method

**1** Combine the yogurt and mustard in a bowl and season with pepper. Stir in the chicken and toss until thoroughly coated.

**2** Put the lettuce, cucumber, celery and grapes into a separate bowl and mix well.

**3** Fold a tortilla in half and in half again to make a cone that is easy to hold. Half-fill the tortilla pocket with the salad mixture and top with some of the chicken mixture. Repeat with the remaining tortillas, salad and chicken. Serve at once.

# traditional roast chicken

## ingredients

**SERVES 4**

25 g/1 oz butter, softened

1 garlic clove,
    finely chopped

3 tbsp finely chopped
    toasted walnuts

1 tbsp chopped
    fresh parsley

salt and pepper

1 oven-ready chicken,
    weighing 1.8 kg/4 lb

1 lime, cut into quarters

2 tbsp vegetable oil

1 tbsp cornflour

2 tbsp water

lime wedges and fresh
    rosemary sprigs,
    to garnish

roast potatoes and a selection
    of freshly cooked
    vegetables, to serve

## method

**1** Mix 1 tablespoon of the butter with the garlic, walnuts and parsley in a small bowl. Season well with salt and pepper. Loosen the skin from the breast of the chicken without breaking it. Spread the butter mixture evenly between the skin and breast meat. Place the lime quarters inside the body cavity.

**2** Pour the oil into a roasting pan. Transfer the chicken to the pan and dot the skin with the remaining butter. Roast in a preheated oven, 190°C/375°F/Gas Mark 5, for 1¾ hours, basting occasionally, until the chicken is tender and the juices run clear when a skewer is inserted into the thickest part of the meat. Lift out the chicken and place on a serving platter to rest for 10 minutes.

**3** Blend the cornflour with the water, then stir into the juices in the pan. Stir over low heat until thickened, adding more water if necessary. Garnish the chicken with lime wedges and rosemary sprigs. Serve with roast potatoes and a selection of freshly cooked vegetables and spoon over the thickened juices.

# chicken pinwheels with blue cheese & herbs

## ingredients

**SERVES 4**

2 tbsp pine nuts, lightly
    toasted

2 tbsp chopped fresh parsley

2 tbsp chopped fresh thyme

1 garlic clove, chopped

1 tbsp grated lemon rind

salt and pepper

4 large, skinless chicken
    breasts

250 g/9 oz blue cheese, such
    as Stilton, crumbled

fresh green and red salad
    leaves, to serve

twists of lemon and sprigs of
    fresh thyme, to garnish

## method

**1** Put the pine nuts into a food processor with the parsley, thyme, garlic and lemon rind. Season with salt and pepper.

**2** Pound the chicken breasts lightly to flatten them. Spread them on one side with the pine nut mixture, then top with the cheese. Roll them up from one short end to the other, so that the filling is enclosed. Wrap the rolls individually in foil and seal well. Transfer to a steamer, or a metal colander placed over a pan of boiling water, cover tightly and steam for 10–12 minutes, or until cooked through.

**3** Arrange the salad leaves on a large serving platter. Remove the chicken from the heat, discard the foil, and cut the chicken rolls into slices. Arrange the slices over the salad leaves, garnish with twists of lemon and sprigs of thyme and serve.

# sticky lime chicken

## ingredients

**SERVES 4**

4 part-boned, skinless
    chicken breasts, about
    140 g/5 oz each
grated rind and juice of 1 lime
1 tbsp honey
1 tbsp olive oil
1 garlic clove, chopped
    (optional)
1 tbsp chopped fresh thyme
pepper
boiled new potatoes and
    lightly cooked seasonal
    vegetables, to serve

## method

**1** Arrange the chicken breasts in a shallow roasting pan.

**2** Put the lime rind and juice, honey, oil, garlic, if using, and thyme in a small bowl and combine thoroughly. Spoon the mixture evenly over the chicken breasts and season with pepper.

**3** Roast the chicken in a preheated oven, 190°C/375°F/Gas Mark 5, basting every 10 minutes, for 35–40 minutes, or until the chicken is tender and the juices run clear when a skewer is inserted into the thickest part of the meat. If the juices still run pink, return the chicken to the oven and cook for a further 5 minutes, then test again. As the chicken cooks, the liquid in the pan thickens to give a tasty, sticky coating.

**4** Serve with boiled new potatoes and lightly cooked seasonal vegetables.

# bacon-wrapped chicken burgers

## ingredients

**SERVES 4**

450 g/1 lb fresh chicken
mince

1 onion, grated

2 garlic cloves, crushed

55 g/2 oz pine nuts, toasted

55 g/2 oz Gruyère cheese,
grated

2 tbsp fresh snipped chives

salt and pepper

2 tbsp wholemeal flour

8 lean bacon slices

1–2 tbsp sunflower oil

crusty rolls, chopped lettuce
and red onion rings,
to serve

mayonnaise and chopped
spring onions (green part
only), to garnish

## method

**1** Place the chicken mince, onion, garlic, pine nuts, cheese, chives and salt and pepper in a food processor. Using the pulse button, blend the mixture together using short sharp bursts. Scrape out onto a board and shape into 4 even-size burgers. Coat in the flour, then cover and chill for 1 hour.

**2** Wrap each burger with 2 bacon slices, securing in place with a wooden cocktail stick.

**3** Heat a heavy-based frying pan and add the oil. When hot, add the burgers and cook over medium heat for 5–6 minutes on each side, or until thoroughly cooked through.

**4** Serve the burgers immediately in crusty rolls on a bed of lettuce and red onion rings and topped with mayonnaise and spring onions.

# chicken fajitas

## ingredients

**SERVES 4**

3 tbsp olive oil, plus extra
    for drizzling

3 tbsp maple syrup or honey

1 tbsp red wine vinegar

2 garlic cloves, crushed

2 tsp dried oregano

1–2 tsp dried
    red pepper flakes

salt and pepper

4 skinless, boneless
    chicken breasts

2 red peppers, deseeded and
    cut into 2.5-cm/1-inch
    strips

8 flour tortillas, warmed

## method

**1** Place the oil, maple syrup, vinegar, garlic, oregano, pepper flakes, salt and pepper in a large, shallow plate or bowl and mix together.

**2** Slice the chicken across the grain into slices 2.5 cm/1 inch thick. Toss in the marinade until well coated. Cover and chill in the refrigerator for 2–3 hours, turning occasionally.

**3** Heat a griddle pan until hot. Lift the chicken slices from the marinade with a slotted spoon, lay on the griddle pan and cook over medium–high heat for 3–4 minutes on each side, or until cooked through. Remove the chicken to a warmed serving plate and keep warm.

**4** Add the peppers, skin-side down, to the griddle pan and cook for 2 minutes on each side. Transfer to the serving plate.

**5** Serve at once with the warmed tortillas to be used as wraps.

# chicken with linguine & artichokes

## ingredients

**SERVES 4**

4 chicken breasts, skinned

finely grated rind and juice of
　　1 lemon

2 tbsp olive oil

2 garlic cloves, crushed

400 g/14 oz canned artichoke
　　hearts, drained and sliced

250 g/9 oz baby plum
　　tomatoes

300 g/10½ oz dried linguine

chopped fresh parsley and
　　finely grated Parmesan
　　cheese, to garnish

## method

**1** Put each chicken breast in turn between 2 pieces of clingfilm and bash with a rolling pin to flatten. Put the chicken into a shallow, non-metallic dish with the lemon rind and juice and 1 tablespoon of the oil and turn to coat in the marinade. Cover and marinate in the refrigerator for 30 minutes.

**2** Heat the remaining oil in a frying pan over low heat, add the garlic and cook for 1 minute, stirring frequently. Add the artichokes and tomatoes and cook for 5 minutes, stirring occasionally. Add about half the marinade from the chicken and cook over medium heat for a further 5 minutes.

**3** Preheat the grill to high. Remove the chicken from the remaining marinade and arrange on the grill pan. Cook the chicken under the preheated grill for 5 minutes each side until thoroughly cooked through. Meanwhile, add the linguine to a saucepan of boiling water and cook for 7–9 minutes, or until just tender.

**4** Drain the pasta and return to the pan, pour over the artichoke and tomato mixture and slice in the cooked chicken.

**5** Divide between 4 warmed plates and sprinkle over the parsley and cheese.

# five-spice chicken with vegetables

## ingredients

**SERVES 4**

2 tbsp sesame oil

1 garlic clove, chopped

3 spring onions, trimmed
    and sliced

1 tbsp cornflour

2 tbsp rice wine

4 skinless chicken breasts,
    cut into strips

1 tbsp Chinese
    five-spice powder

1 tbsp grated fresh ginger

125 ml/4 fl oz chicken stock

100 g/3½ oz baby corn cobs,
    sliced

300 g/10½ oz beansprouts

finely chopped spring onions,
    to garnish, optional

freshly cooked jasmine rice,
    to serve

## method

**1** Heat the oil in a preheated wok or large frying pan. Add the garlic and spring onions and stir-fry over medium–high heat for 1 minute.

**2** In a bowl, mix together the cornflour and rice wine, then add the mixture to the pan. Stir-fry for 1 minute, then add the chicken, five-spice powder, ginger and chicken stock and cook for another 4 minutes. Add the corn cobs and cook for 2 minutes, then add the beansprouts and cook for another minute.

**3** Remove from the heat, garnish with chopped spring onions, if using, and serve with freshly cooked jasmine rice.

# chicken chow mein

## ingredients

**SERVES 4**

250 g/9 oz medium egg
  noodles

2 tbsp sunflower oil

280 g/10 oz cooked chicken
  breasts, shredded

1 garlic clove, finely chopped

1 red pepper, deseeded
  and thinly sliced

100 g/3½ oz shiitake
  mushrooms, sliced

6 spring onions, sliced

100 g/3½ oz beansprouts

3 tbsp soy sauce

1 tbsp sesame oil

## method

**1** Place the egg noodles in a large bowl or dish and break them up slightly. Pour enough boiling water over the noodles to cover and let stand while preparing the other ingredients.

**2** Preheat a wok over medium heat. Add the sunflower oil and swirl it around to coat the sides of the wok. When the oil is hot, add the shredded chicken, garlic, pepper, mushrooms, spring onions and beansprouts to the wok and stir-fry for about 5 minutes.

**3** Drain the noodles thoroughly then add them to the wok, toss well, and stir-fry for a further 5 minutes. Drizzle the soy sauce and sesame oil over the chow mein and toss until well combined.

**4** Transfer the chicken chow mein to warmed serving bowls and serve immediately.

# risotto alla milanese

## ingredients

**SERVES 4**

125 g/4¹/₂ oz butter

900 g/2 lb skinless, boneless
   chicken breasts, thinly
   sliced

1 large onion, chopped

500 g/1 lb 2 oz Arborio rice

150 ml/5 fl oz white wine

1 tsp crushed saffron threads

salt and pepper

600 ml/1 pint simmering
   chicken stock

fresh flat-leaf parsley sprigs,
   to garnish

55 g/2 oz Parmesan cheese
   shavings, to serve

## method

**1** Melt 55 g/2 oz of the butter in a deep frying pan. Add the chicken and onion and cook over medium heat, stirring occasionally, for 8–10 minutes, until golden brown.

**2** Reduce the heat, add the rice and cook, stirring constantly, for a few minutes until the grains begin to swell and are thoroughly coated in the butter.

**3** Add the wine and saffron and season with salt and pepper. Cook, stirring constantly, until the wine has completely evaporated. Add 2 ladlefuls of the hot stock and cook, stirring constantly, until it has been completely absorbed. Add the remaining stock, 1 ladleful at a time, stirring constantly and allowing each ladleful to be absorbed before adding the next, until all the stock has been absorbed and the rice has a creamy texture – this will take 20–25 minutes.

**4** Garnish each individual plate with a parsley sprig, then serve the risotto immediately, sprinkled with the Parmesan cheese shavings and dotted with the remaining butter.

This edition published by Parragon Books Ltd in 2013
LOVE FOOD is an imprint of Parragon Books Ltd

Parragon Books Ltd
Chartist House
15–17 Trim Street
Bath BA1 1HA, UK
www.parragon.com/lovefood

ISBN 978-1-4723-2234-0

Printed in China

**Notes for the Reader**
This book uses both metric and imperial measurements. Follow the same units of measurement throughout; do not mix metric and imperial. All spoon measurements are level: teaspoons are assumed to be 5 ml, and tablespoons are assumed to be 15 ml. Unless otherwise stated, milk is assumed to be full fat, eggs and individual vegetables are medium, and pepper is freshly ground black pepper. Unless otherwise stated, all root vegetables should be washed in plain water and peeled prior to using.

For best results, use a food thermometer when cooking meat and poultry – check the latest government guidelines for current advice.

Garnishes, decorations and serving suggestions are all optional and not necessarily included in the recipe ingredients or method.

The times given are an approximate guide only. Preparation times differ according to the techniques used by different people and the cooking times may also vary from those given. Optional ingredients, variations or serving suggestions have not been included in the time calculations.

Recipes using raw or very lightly cooked eggs should be avoided by infants, the elderly, pregnant women, convalescents and anyone suffering from an illness. Pregnant and breastfeeding women are advised to avoid eating peanuts and peanut products. Sufferers from nut allergies should be aware that some of the ready-made ingredients used in the recipes in this book may contain nuts. Always check the packaging before use.